KINGSTON IN THE FIFT

PLANS *for a new-look Kingston were drawn up in the 1930s but the Second World War brought everything to a halt. When the war finally ended, there was a longing for a new beginning. Fine old landmarks were pulled down to make way for the new. Shops, offices and high-rise buildings sprung up on many a historic corner. In hindsight, some were no less than eyesores. However, though Kingston was starting to change architecturally, few could have guessed that the 1950s spelt the gradual beginning of the end for industries that still dominated the local economy but which would vanish over the next three decades. The greatest change was to be along the riverside. In the Fifties, it was still industrial. Today, there is a fine promenade and cafes in place of wharfs, cranes and warehouses. Most of the pictures in this book have rarely been seen before. They came from hundreds of glass negatives offered to June Sampson two decades ago. She has carefully archived them over the years with the help of Stephen Day and presented them to Kingston Museum and Heritage Centre. In collaboration with Mark Davison, some of these striking images can now be shared with the people of Kingston, past and present, through the pages of this book.*

Acknowledgments

Stephen Day, Kingston Museum and Heritage Centre, Jill Lamb, Emma Rummins, Keith Hathaway, Sean Duggan and Hilton Tims. A special thanks to the Surrey Comet, which has reported on Kingston's people and events since 1854 and is now one of our most valuable local history resources.

Photographic credits

Sampson/Day collection, Surrey Comet, Mark Davison collection.

**Published by Mark Davison
North Bank, Smoke Lane, Reigate,
Surrey RH2 7HJ.
Telephone: 01737 221215
e-mail: mark.davison1@virgin.net**

Printed by Litho Techniques, Godstone Road, Whyteleafe, Surrey CR3 0EA

**First edition November 2008
Copyright 2008
Reprinted November 2009**

ISBN 978-0-9543759-2-8

The Old Curiosity Shop, High Street, being prepared for demolition in November 1953.

The Mayor of Kingston, Councillor D.M. Alexander, takes the salute at the Remembrance Day parade through Market Place in November 1957. The Midland Bank, on the right, is now a pizza restaurant.

Front cover photograph: Clarence Street seen from Kingston Bridge in the 1950s. Thames Street emerges on the right and continues on the left. Thirty years later, all the buildings, save Bentalls' frontage, were demolished and replaced by the John Lewis development and part of the ring-road.
Back cover photograph: Fashionable young ladies at Surbiton Lagoon in August 1953.

In the 1950s and 1960s, people would queue all night for Bentalls' annual winter and summer sales. This picture of the throng in July 1955 shows Bentalls' Clarence Street frontage, demolished in 1990 to make way for the Bentall Centre. The shops in the distance, beyond Wood Street, went in 1986 to make way for the John Lewis department store – opened in 1990 – and part of the relief road.

Invasion of the motor car in Kingston – and the arrival of parking meters

MOTORISTS in the 1950s could still drive into Kingston town centre and park in any available kerbside gap without payment or punishment.

This wasn't the idyll it might seem, however.

The fact was that Kingston was clogging up with cars parked on both sides of every road at a time when one-way streets had yet to be introduced.

There were alternatives. For instance, in 1925, Kingston Council had built its first "public motor park" on the west side of Eden Street with the aim of "reducing the congestion of stationary cars in the streets" by offering all-day parking for sixpence (two-and-a-half pence in today's currency).

But the council promised that the new amenity would not put an end to street parking.

"No one wants to drive trade away, and no one could cavil at a car stopping in the Market Place for half-an-hour or so," said a spokesman.

Leonard Bentall, head of the famous department store in Kingston, provided the second covered car park in 1928, and the council later opened a third in Fairfield North.

But still people preferred to park for nothing in the streets. And the council was reluctant to stop them in case it drove shoppers from the town.

In 1937, Kingston Chamber of Commerce, with remarkable foresight, suggested easing congestion with a one-way system.

It also called on the council to entice

The Horsefair, formerly covered by homes, shops and pubs, was levelled in the 1930s and its residents evicted without redress, for a scheme that, due to the Second World War, never materialised. The site became a temporary car park until the 1980s, when construction of John Lewis and the final stretch of the relief road began on the land. The buildings in the background on the right were also demolished as part of the project.

drivers into the car parks by making them free. However, the Second World War put the matter on hold, and, by the 1950s, the problem had gone from bad to worse.

In 1953, Venners, of New Malden, introduced its "Park-O-Meter", the first machine of its kind to be produced in Britain, and it was successfully put on trial in London.

The Surrey Comet explained the new gadget: "Motorists will draw up beside a meter, place a coin in the slot and be allowed to park for the time shown on the dial. At the end of an hour, or two hours, according to whether sixpence, or a shilling, is inserted, a large red tab, bearing the word 'expired' will appear on the dial."

Motorists exceeding their time would pay an excess charge at the nearest police station, or be fined if they failed to do so.

It was 1961 before Kingston Council decided to adopt meters – only to rescind the decision soon afterwards.

The Comet was outraged at the U-turn. In a prominent comment piece it said: "In

Kingston, there is the absurd situation that a few motorists are able to occupy free the limited amount of kerbside parking space while others must pay for the accommodation in nearby car parks."

"The introduction of meters will remove that anomaly, forcing the all-day parkers into the cheap parks on the fringe of town, and leaving the kerbside available to shoppers."

Kingston Council the following year reluctantly gave in to the introduction of meters.

Saturday congestion in Wood Street on 12th December 1953. The car park partly visible on the left is now covered by John Lewis, which opened in 1990. Beyond it is a distant view of Bentalls' car park and garage, which was replaced in 1969, only to be demolished in 1988 for today's Bentall Centre parking complex.

View of the Eden Street junction, looking towards London Road on a winter's day in 1957. The buildings beyond the Wheelwrights Arms (right) survived into the 21st Century, apart from the Lewis tobacconist's shop – noted for its cigars. The adjoining shop, now Games, is being purpose-built for the Kay Morley fashion store.

Tower blocks built to ease problems

Post-war housing crisis

THE decade following the Second World War saw a maelstrom of change in and around Kingston, especially on the construction front. In the town centre, familiar old landmarks were razed to make way for new ones and, further afield, council estates were profoundly altering the landscape. These new homes were sorely needed, for Kingston faced a serious housing shortage at the end of the war. One reason was that many homes had been bomb damaged or destroyed and the onus was on Kingston and Council to rehouse those who had been displaced.

Another reason was the soaring demand as service personnel, many of them newly married, returned home from the war.

The only solution was to install people in requisitioned houses, or temporary huts, until building restrictions and shortage of material had eased and building projects could begin.

The first major scheme began in 1949, when Kingston Council opened Cambridge Gardens on what had been the site of the mansion and landscaped grounds of the Cambridge Home for soldiers' widows in Norbiton. Comprising 160 flats, it was the largest block in Surrey at that time.

The elegant slopes of Kingston Hill were next in line, where 120 flats were completed at Cumberland Lodge by 1953.

The following year saw the completion of 320 homes on the site of Kingsnympton Hall, the home of an Indian prince until its destruction by bombs.

These, plus several other developments, meant that by 1956, Kingston Council had built 361 houses and 879 flats and many more would follow in the year ahead.

There were some early disputes with residents at the Kingsnympton Estate over them being charged a shilling a week for gas in the communal laundry room. Tenants boycotted the laundry and did it themselves, hanging out washing all over the estate and on trees.

As the Surrey Comet put it: ". . .battle banners in the form of petticoats were hoisted by housewives."

The east side of Clarence Street and Eden Street junction was demolished in 1957-9 for much-needed road widening. This picture, taken in 1957, just before the work began, shows on the right Mence Smith's Household Stores at 56-58 Clarence Street. Adjoining it, on the corner of Weston Park, is the Wheelwrights Arms, so-called because it originated as a wheelwright's shop which was converted into a beerhouse and then replaced by a handsome pub with a forecourt fronting Clarence Street. The pub was also demolished for road widening and replaced by smaller premises with an entrance round the corner in Weston Park.

This view of Eden Street in 1957 will evoke memories for many people. All the buildings on the left, including the picturesque Three Compasses pub, were pulled down in 1977 to make way for the second stage of the Eden Walk shopping centre. The Post Office, right, closed in 1997. But the empty building, opened in 1876 and protected by listing, was still awaiting a new purpose in 2008. The Victorian shop buildings beyond also avoided the bulldozer but the handsome Methodist church, built in 1890 and demolished in 1964, is now replaced by a shop and offices.

Eden Street looking south from Clarence Street in February 1957. Most of the buildings on the left would soon disappear. But the handsome bank in the far right foreground still survives. Originally designed for National Provincial in 1925, it is now home to HSBC. The overhead wires vanished in 1962 when trolleybuses were replaced by buses – mainly Routemasters.

Lilley & Skinner shoe shop at 47-49 Clarence Street in April 1957. Recessed shopfronts, so fashionable then, are a thing of the past now, as soaring shop rents mean all possible space must be given over to selling. The bus stop is for the trolleybus numbers 604 and 605 to New Malden and Wimbledon. It was in 1957 that all forms of rationing, introduced during the war, finally ended.

A lorry crash in Clarence Street in 1958. The view is looking west towards Kingston Bridge. The street then had two-way traffic. In 1989 it was pedestrianised, following completion of the relief road.

The Clarence Street end of Eden Street on a bright February day in 1957. The YMCA and Bonsor Stevens Estate Agents' properties were demolished in 1988 to make way for Adams Walk, which opened in 1990.

Christmas shoppers queue outside Bentalls in December 1953. Note the dress code of the time – no trainers, tracksuits, anoraks or baseball caps; short trousers and long socks for pre-teen boys; tailored "princess"- style coats for little girls; and ladies seldom wore trousers save at home or on holiday.

Bentalls had some customer luxuries that have not survived to the present day. There was a spacious ladies' lounge where shoppers could relax on comfy chairs and sofas; or freshen up with face powder from bowls on the mirrored dressing tables.

A housewife selects her Christmas turkey in December 1953. The large English chickens in the front are 7s 6d (just over 35p) each, and the smaller ones on the left are 6s (30p). Sausages are on offer at 2s 6d (half a crown, or just over 12p) per pound. The shop is not named, but is probably Follet's in Kingston Market Place – now Kew Fashions.

Customers came from miles around for variety of stores

Christmas shopping

KINGSTON in the 1950s was in the grip of a planning blight inflicted by the Second World War which caused improvement schemes drawn up in the 1930s to be put on hold for the next four decades. Nevertheless, it was still widely regarded as the Thames Valley's best shopping centre, drawing customers from many miles away.

This was particularly evident in the run-up to Christmas 1953, when such an unprecedented number of shoppers poured in by bus, coach and train, that the Surrey Comet conducted a street poll to discover why.

Shoppers gave four main reasons: the variety of shops (more than in places such as Croydon, Sutton and Guildford); "exciting" window displays; good public tranport into the town; and the bargains to be had in the Market Place. But then, as now, Christmas parking was problematic.

"By 10am the pavements were thick with pedestrians and the streets choked with motorists vainly looking for somewhere to park," reported the Comet. "Every street had cars nose to tail. In High Street before ten o'clock the lines stretched on both sides of the road as far as Town End Wharf, the parks by then already being full."

The town could boast two prestigious department stores. One was Hides, which had been trading in the Market Place since 1760 (it closed in 1986). The other was Bentalls, founded in 1867, and still going strong.

There was also a greater variety of shops than now, especially in thoroughfares such as Thames Street, Castle Street and Fife Road, which were almost retail villages in their own right.

How the broadsheet Surrey Comet appeared in 1953.

A demonstrator of new products astonishes children and their parents with this juggling trick using bubbles at a Christmas promotion in Bentalls' department store on 12th December 1953.

A characterful stallholder in Kingston promotes tea-towels on 12th December 1953 while a shopper holds pound notes at the ready to buy.

Church Street in November 1957. The mock Tudor building on the left was the Surrey Comet's head office until 1984. Its shopfront was hand-carved from the timbers of ancient fighting ships brought from Portsmouth.

Mackney's store in Fife Road holds a closing down sale in June 1959. The business shut upon the owner's retirement. The gabled premises are now home to Marks & Spencer's menswear and homeware departments. There were no parking restrictions in the road in the 1950s. All the buildings in the picture survived into the 21st century.

LADIES' & GIRLS'

FROCKS

You will find a splendid
selection in all sizes

•

MACKNEYS
LTD.

FIFE ROAD   KINGSTON 0088

Mackney's store, Fife Road, announces it is to close down in July 1959. Mackney's was founded in 1898 by John Mackney and served local families for more than 60 years. It was a type of unpretentious emporium, selling a large variety of amateurishly displayed merchandise that was common in Britain in the 1950s but has now disappeared. There were men's, women's and children's wear plus corsetry, carpets and household textiles. Many were shocked when it shut on 4th July 1959. Inset: A 1953 advertisement in the Surrey Comet.

The Kay Morley fashion store in Weston Park in June 1956, just before its owner had demolished and replaced it with new premises.

Parked cars in Fife Road in September 1955.

Old houses in St James' Road, near The Guildhall, are pulled down in 1957 to make way for the new County Court, opened in 1961.

Kingston Bus Station, Clarence Street, in April 1955. It and the adjoining cinema were demolished in 2000 and The Rotunda opened in their place in 2002. The large building rearing over the railway bridge and station is the Three Fishes pub, later renamed the Royal Charter. It was demolished in the 1980s to make way for the relief road.

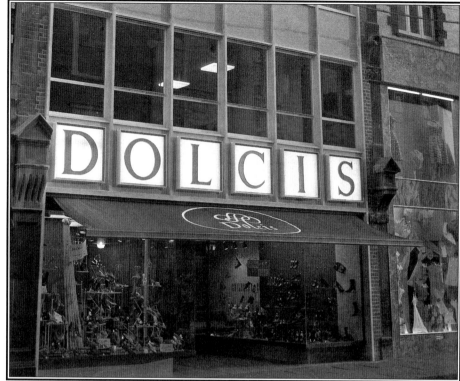

Left: *Gaydon's, of Thames Street, had traded as a jeweller's and watchmaker's in Kingston for 118 years when the business finally closed in 1982. The shop's best-loved feature was its handsome street clock – Kingston's favourite trysting place for many decades. After Gaydon's move to Clarence Street in 1956, the clock was transferred to Fife Road, where it remains. Gaydon's Thames Street premises is now home to the Royal Bank of Scotland. This picture was taken in 1955.*
Above: *Dolcis shoe shop had been in Clarence Street for 92 years when the entire Dolcis chain – started by a street trader in 1863 – collapsed in 2008 and the Kingston premises were acquired by Optical Express and Carphone Warehouse. This photograph is dated April 1957. Cuffs fashion store, can partly be seen on the right of Gaydon's. See page 48.*

The Temperance Billiard Hall, Times Furnishing, and Stuart Radio Ltd in Fife Road in January 1955. This new Times Furnishing building, in the utilitarian style that was to become all too common in the 1960s, replaced the former Royal County Theatre and opened in 1955. The furnishing store has long since gone but the premises continued into the 21st Century as Sports World. Its neighbours were razed and the sites redeveloped. The theatre was Kingston's first when it opened in 1897. It shut in 1912 and became the Super Cinema but failed to live up to its name. The premises were gutted in 1940. It then lay empty for 14 years. The buildings on the left were later demolished to make way for Dolphin Street and part of the Bentall Centre.

Left and above, A threatened rail strike in 1953 prompted panic posting by people anxious to despatch Christmas cards and parcels before rail transport became paralysed. To cope with the rush, Kingston's central Post Office took on 600 temporary workers, who toiled alongside regular staff to establish a record in the amount of mail handled that week.

A spotless Kingston Hospital and nurses immaculately dressed

BACK in the 1950s, Kingston Hospital's nurses wore cotton dresses topped by white starched aprons. Their hair was neatly groomed under white starched caps – or hats, as they were known in the profession.

This clothing was washed daily in the hospital laundry, and never worn beyond the hospital boundaries.

Today, nurses can be seen shopping or on public transport in Kingston, still wearing their uniforms – something that would not have been tolerated in those days.

Now, staff wear dresses, or tunics and trousers, which are often worn repeatedly without washing. Nurses say this is because hospitals no longer provide them with a free laundry service.

These fine ward pictures, dating from July 1953 – the year of the Queen's coronation – were taken by the Surrey Comet to mark the expansion of the maternity services at Kingston Hospital, following the closure of the maternity department at Surbiton Hospital, in Ewell Road.

The Surbiton ward had only 11 beds, whereas the new Kingston ward had 17, bringing the hospital's total to 100.

The new accommodation was mainly for the patients of local GPs. Hospital cases went to two other wards.

The unit stayed empty in its first week. Then came a rush, with all beds becoming occupied and fully booked until the following March.

The Comet reported at the time: "The first impression of the visitor is the cheerful atmosphere, engendered first by the welcome extended by the sister-in-charge and then the warmth of delicately tinted pink walls.

"The whole unit is on one floor. It comprises a ward with 10 beds, another with four, and three single-ward beds. These could be called private rooms, and are used in cases when it is necessary that the mother should be alone."

The babies lay in labelled cots in a nursery, divided from the corridor by a glass partition, so nurses could keep an eye on them. There was also a babies' bathroom, with special shallow sinks.

The Comet was impressed by the fact that the mothers' beds boasted interior sprung mattresses, and that each bed had its own table and special "railways" that enabled curtains to be pulled round the bed in complete silence.

It reported: "The system follows the most modern methods in mid-wifery, and mothers are kept in the ward for 14 days, unless there is a heavy demand for beds."

The matron, a Miss McIntyre, was allowed the last word in the Comet's write-up.

She said: "We do try to keep abreast of the modern methods. We aim high."

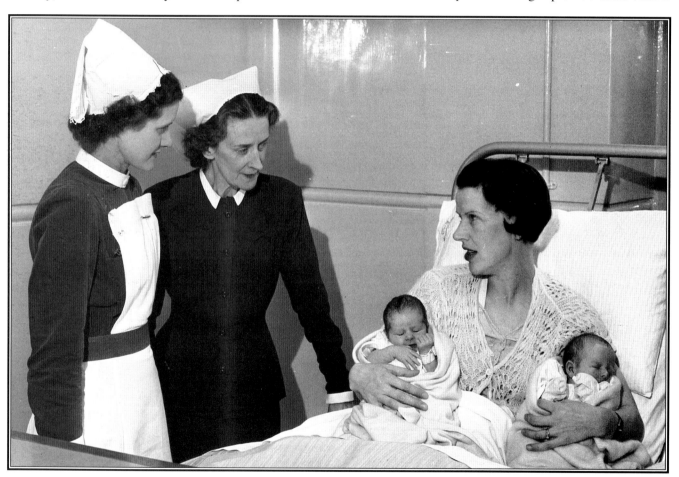

Mrs Olwen Ashfield, of Salisbury Road, New Malden, proudly nurses her new-born twins, David and Marion, in Kingston Hospital's new maternity unit in the summer of 1953. With her are Sister Burbridge, left, and the matron, Miss Mcintyre.

The cheerful new maternity wing at Kingston Hospital in July 1953. These days, flowers are banned from many hospitals for fear the water they stand in harbours germs.

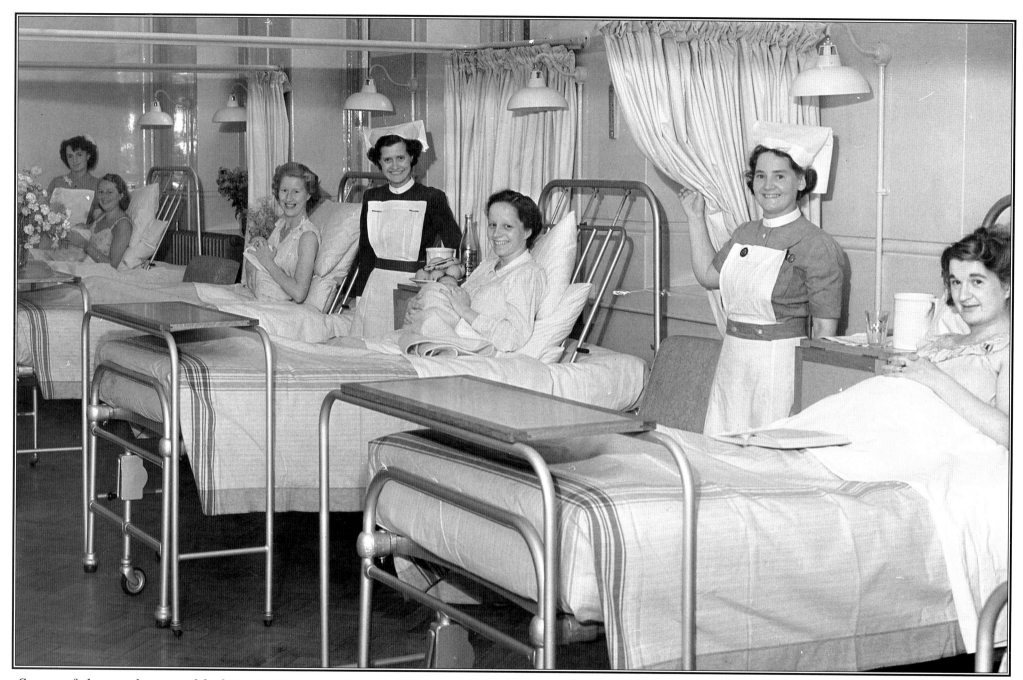

Some of the mothers and babies in Kingston Hospital's new maternity ward in July 1953 when it was still normal practice for women to stay in bed for a fortnight after giving birth. Now, they are often discharged the same day.

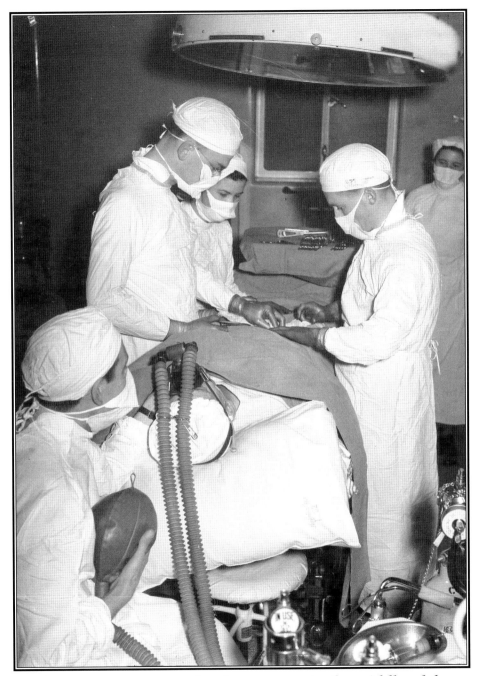

An emergency operation in progress in the middle of the night at Kingston Hospital in January 1954.

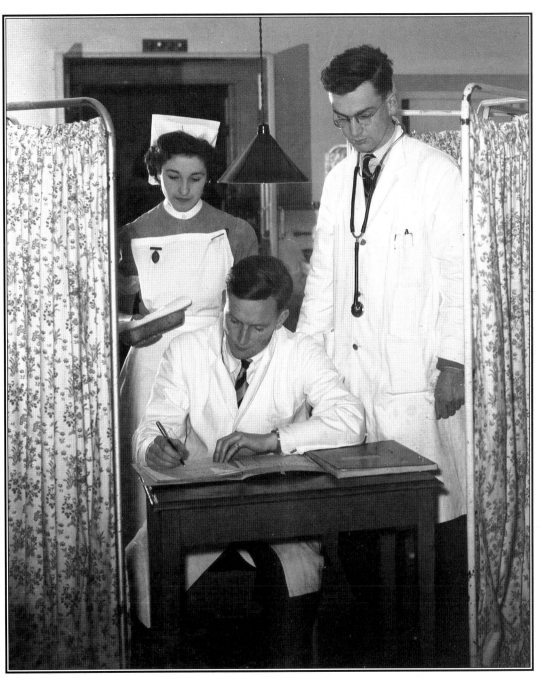

A medical team completes some paperwork in a ward at Kingston Hospital in January 1954.

Industrial action by workers

We're on strike!

IF KINGSTON's young residents of today were taken back in time to the 1950s, they would probably be surprised to learn that the Royal borough was an important industrial centre, with some 30 per cent of the local workforce engaged in manufacturing.

A major employer was Hawker Aircraft, later British Aerospace. Others included Decca, Vine Products, Celestion, Bradbury Wilkinson, Venner (pioneers of time switches and parking meters), Arrow Plastics and many more.

The 1950s also saw a rise in trade union militancy.

Thus Kingston, with its plethora of factories, became accustomed to the sight of protesting workers taking to the streets, or gathering on the Fairfield, or at the Cattle Market – which really was a livestock market then, not just the bus station and car park it is now.

This was most apparent at the start of 1957 when it emerged that Hawker would have to sack 2,000 workers.

This catastrophic news followed a Government decision to cancel an order for a hundred of the Hunter jet fighters designed by Sydney Camm and his Kingston team, and in which Neville Duke had broken the world air speed record in 1953.

The situation was grim. Seven hundred workers had already been dismissed the previous year because of a falling off in Hunter orders. And though the company had plans for another new fighter designed by Camm, it was not due to fly until mid-1958.

Trade union and trades council members joined in a strike in the mid-Fifties through Kingston. A long stream of protestors can be seen here passing under the Richmond Road railway bridge. In the distance, towering up, is the Regal Cinema which in latter years became a bingo hall.

To draw attention to their plight, the men organised a mass march in January 1957, starting from the Hawker factory in Richmond Road and proceeding to the Fairfield to meet up with colleagues from the firm's other works in Canbury Park Road, Kingston. They marched to the Guildhall to petition the mayor for an official enquiry into the effect the dismissals would have on the town.

In February, the first 150 sackings took place.

Those with five or more years of service were given two weeks' notice, the rest one week. It was also announced that of Hawker's four factories, Langley would close and Blackpool would be run down.

But despair turned to jubilation a few months later with an order from the Indian government for 200 Hunters.

The contract was signed on 31st August 1957 and work began the very next day – a Sunday.

It was the biggest export order ever for a British plane, worth £30 million, ensuring three years of continuous production and more jobs for hundreds of workers.

It transpired that negotiations had been going on for more than two years against fierce competition for the contract from the makers of the French Mystere plane.

The Surrey Comet reported that all the aircraft for India would be made at Kingston, where Hawker was also completing Hunter orders for the Dutch and Danish governments.

"Only a few months ago, the future looked bleak due to defence cuts, and there were suggestions that the factory be diverted to civil aircraft," the Comet reported, adding: "The management always had faith in the Hunter, and believed it would attract foreign orders. Now that faith has been justified.

"Meanwhile, work is going on in the development of the new supersonic strike aircraft, P1121, designed by Sydney Camm, and being produced as a private venture at this stage."

One of several other industrial disputes in Kingston during the Fifties was in 1953. In December of that year, the Confederation of Shipbuilders and Engineering Unions called on its 25,000 members to strike for a day after their demand for a 15 per cent wage increase had been refused.

In Kingston, about 90 per cent of engineers answered the call.

All factory gates were picketed by union members, and several hundred gathered at Kingston Cattle Market to give a unanimous pledge of support for any further calls for action.

Strikers from Hawker's Kingston factory march though the Market Place in January 1957.

Industrial strife in Kingston's workplaces

About 400 workers gathered at Kingston Cattle Market on 2nd December 1953 as part of a one-day strike by engineers across Britain demanding a 15% pay rise. In the background is one of Kingston's earliest car parks, a basic affair put up some 30 years earlier.

Faced with what seemed like certain ruin, Hawker workers amass at Fairfield in 1957 to listen to their union leaders.

Faced with dismissal after the Government slashed a big order for Hunter fighter planes in 1957, Hawker Aircraft workers begin a protest from the firm's Richmond Road factory. Soon, the main road frontage of the Hawker's building, seen here, would be replaced. See page 36.

Aggrieved Hawker's employees march through Market Place in January 1957.

The newly rebuilt Hawker factory in Richmond Road in December 1958. It was demolished in 1992 and replaced by a housing estate.

Clarence Street in the autumn of 1954. The following year the Empire Theatre closed to become a supermarket (it is now a Lloyds No 1 Bar) and the Elite Cinema was demolished for the building of a C&A store (now Wilkinsons).

A 603 trolleybus destined for Tolworth enters Clarence Street from London Road in 1953. Ahead is the Century Elite Cinema. Adjoining it on the right is Farebrothers, now the site of a Travelodge Hotel, and on the left the Granada Cinema, now the Oceana nightclub.

End of an era in cinema history

The Elite's demise

THE picture on the previous page shows a busy scene in Kingston town centre in 1953. Trolley bus wires criss-cross the skyline where London Road merges with Clarence Street.

In the centre of the photograph is the Elite Cinema. – briefly renamed The Century. It was first opened on 21st May 1921.

It closed on New Year's Day 1955 with the showing of Modern Times and Go Man Go. The cinema was demolished and the site redeveloped. C&A later occupied the corner site.

On the day this 1953 photograph was taken, the film The Wages of Fear was being screened.

The story centred around the manager of a Central American oilfield who offered big money to drivers who would take nitro-glycerine into the jungle to put out an oil well blaze. The film was described as a "great suspense thriller".

The picture on this page shows the demolition team pulling down the remains of The Elite in March 1955.

When The Elite was first opened, its owners declared: "Today, the great and powerful picture-going public demand a fittingly graceful and enduring portal to their wonderland, made royal-rich and cosy by all the thousand and one available devices with a charmed sense of remoteness from the workaday throng. And this, for Kingston upon Thames, is now accomplished."

The Elite originally had its own orchestra plus a superb pipe organ,

Demolition of the Century Elite Cinema in March 1955. In those days there were no health and safety regulations to protect workmen or passers-by. All the buildings on the right were later replaced by new shops and flats.

acquired from a stately home in Derby and expensively rebuilt and augmented by Lewis & Co., one of the most acclaimed organ makers of the 19th and 20th centuries.

Also in the picture, opposite, is the 603 trolley bus, bound for the terminus at the Red Lion, Tolworth. Its route would include Richmond Road, Kings Road, London Road and Eden Street.

Trolleybuses ran from 1931 to May 1962 on the former tram routes. It was a sad day on 8th May 1962 when a special trolleybus marked the end of an era by making the last journey into Kingston from Fulwell depot.

Hundreds lined the streets to witness the historic moment when the decorated bus passed.

Closure of Kingston's Empire Theatre and The Elite Cinema

MARCH 16th 1955 was a sad day for Kingston. This was the date the Kingston Empire closed, and with it a chapter of local theatrical history that had lasted nearly 45 years. A sorrowful director, Mr W.L. Hodges concluded that the people of the town did not want a theatre any more.

The theatre opened on 24th October, 1910. Some 2,000 people packed the auditorium, while outside hundreds more jostled on the pavement, hoping vainly for seats at the second performance.

It was to stay that way for years. "Packed From Head to Ceiling" became the Empire's catchphrase, and once theatre-goers had to book well ahead for a seat at either of the twice-nightly shows.

Clarence Sounes, the Empire's first owner and manager, was adamant that his theatre would not be of the bawdy London type.

"No effort will be spared to avoid anything the least offensive to the most sensitive," he declared. "The performances will be kept entirely free from any suggestion of coarseness.

"The slightest attempt at vulgarity will be immediately suppressed. In fact, it will be my greatest endeavour to make this a family resort where parents can bring their children with the greatest confidence."

The opening programme was headed by the Great Raymond, described by the Surrey Comet as a "conjurist and illusionist of marked ability".

From that time on, the Empire was a magnet for every big name in British showbusiness, and from overseas as well. The stars included jazz trumpeter Louis Armstrong, who played there for a week.

The building also launched one of the best-known stars of the theatre – Noel Coward. He was a small boy when he was taken from his home in Teddington to see the Empire's pantomime.

The Elite's auditorium in the final stages of demolition in March 1955.

"It was my first ever visit to a theatre and I decided there and then to make it my career," he said in later years. "Actually I never saw the panto. The excitement made me sick. But it set the course of my life."

The taste for variety entertainment waned after the Second World War and the Empire was one of several theatres to close in the 1950s.

The Empire's final show was La Vie Parisienne, a revue starring local comedian Sonny Jenks.

Kingston Council lost a chance to turn the premises into a new civic hall and concert venue. Instead, the old theatre was gutted and became a Premier Supermarket in 1956. More recently it became home to Lloyds No 1 bar, operated by Wetherspoons. Happily, the old handsome frontage in Clarence Street survived into the new millennium.

Though 1950s Kingston had fallen out of love with its theatre, it was still enamoured with its Elite Cinema.

There was therefore universal regret when it was demolished in March 1955, the month the Empire closed.

It wasn't because there was a shortage of local cinemas. As well as the Elite, Kingston town centre had four others – the Granada, Kingston Kinema, the Odeon and the Regal.

There were also two in Surbiton – the Odeon in Claremont Road and the Ritz on St Mark's Hill– plus Odeons on Tolworth (where Tolworth Tower was built in the early 1960s) and Shannon Corner, New Malden.

What made the Elite so special was its architecture. It was a truly beautiful landmark, with a frontage that curved round the London Road and Clarence Street corner, and boasted six fine classical stone columns.

It opened in 1921 as what its owners described as "a lordly pleasure house wherein at ease one may participate in the larger life of the screen."

The foyer was panelled with oak from Preston Hall, a period mansion in Kent, as were the coffee room and four tea lounges on the first floor.

The Elite, designed by architects Adamson and Kinns, seated 1,400 and was opened by the Elite (Kingston) Picture Theatre Ltd in May 1921.

In 1946, it was bought by Granada, who seven years previously had opened a cinema next door – The Granada, then re-named its new purchase the Century, the name it customarily gave to its second cinema in a town.

This caused such an outcry that Kingston Council persuaded the company to compromise by renaming it the Century Elite.

The Century Elite closed on 1st January 1955, after Granada had sold it to C&A Modes.

The building was demolished in March 1955 – the same month The Empire closed – to make way for an unlovely C&A department store that in recent times became a branch of Wilkinson's.

This picture was taken in February 1956 when C&A was nearing completion. Beyond it, on the left, is the Granada Cinema, which opened in 1939, was converted into a complex of three cinemas, Options night club and a restaurant in 1987, and given over entirely to the Oceana night club in 2002.

Fifties' riverside

Eagle Wharf in 1955. Now its site is a paved park, fronted by part of a mile-long riverside walk started in 1856 and completed in 2003.

ANYONE travelling back in time to the 1950s would probably be struck most by the riverside. It was, so dramatically and utterly different from now.

The Victorians had created Canbury Gardens at the northern end of the town, and Queen's Promenade at the south. Otherwise, the river frontage was still monopolised by industry, with no public access.

The picture on this page shows Eagle Wharf, half a century ago. Today it is a small paved park where people sit and watch the Thames flow by.

In the 1950s, it was covered by the erstwhile Eagle Brewery, which ceased production in the 1920s, and was later acquired by G.J. Palmer & Son, specialists in "seaborne" coal – coal shipped direct from British collieries to Kingston by specially chartered ships.

The original brewery building was handsome, but during Palmer's tenure, it was stripped of its elegant turrets and other embellishments to make way for the cranes needed to unload cargoes of coal.

Palmers had gone by the 1960s and the building was demolished early in the 1970s.

To its left was the Ram public house's beer garden, which separated Eagle Wharf from Palmer's other depot on Pioneer Wharf. And adjoining Pioneer Wharf was the Odeon cinema, which backed on to the river. The Ram's garden survives, but Pioneer Wharf is now the site of offices, shops and bar of Eagle House.

The Odeon was demolished in 1988 and eventually replaced by the Rose Theatre, which opened in 2008. The cinema had first opened on 3rd July 1933 with a showing of Monte Carlo and One Good Turn. It closed on 15th July 1967 with a screening of The Great Escape.

Kingston Power Station in March 1957. In the foreground is the Steadfast Sea Cadets Corps' HQ and part of the Turk's boat-building premises – both subsequently demolished. The power station closed in 1980 and was demolished for housing in 1994.

The Thames at Kingston in the 1950s was still of industrial as well as leisure importance – as shown in this picture of leisure craft sailing past the cranes and coal yards on Eagle Wharf in March 1957.

A regatta scene in 1957. The steps led to a riverside garden created for Nuthalls restaurant in 1904, and now part of the public riverside walk. On the left is part of Kingston Tannery which burned down in 1963 after 300 years in the town.

Familiar shouting in the streets

Barrow boys

NOWADAYS, Kingston town centre vibrates with an electronically amplified din from street "musicians" or the roar from passing cars with windows down and a thumping rap song playing at full blast.

Street noise was part of life in the 1950s, too. But then it came mainly from newspaper sellers, shouting their time-honoured pleas to "read all about it," and barrow boys bawling out their wares wherever they could find a pitch.

There were street musicians and cars, too, of course.

But as the former performed without electronic aids, and few of the motor cars had radios, their output of decibels was nothing compared to now.

Nevertheless, there was a mounting tide of complaints against barrow boys shouting out their custom.

They had done so from time immemorial, but by 1953, there were so many of them, and their noise was deemed so disturbing, that Kingston Council took up a new bylaw. This made barrow boys who "cause annoyance by shouting" liable to a fine of £5, with a similar penalty for those who left litter.

The Surrey Comet reported that the barrow boys' bawling caused "great annoyance" to office workers, adding that the offenders' main centre of operation was outside the Garden of Remembrance and in Union Street.

"Fines for obstruction have done nothing to curb the activities of these itinerant vendors," said the Comet's leader column in August 1953. "Perhaps if court action is taken under the new

Barrow boys selling fruit and vegetables in Church Street, Kingston, in 1957. Behind them is the Surrey Comet's former HQ. Its mock-Tudor frontage, created in 1927 from ancient ship timbers, still survives on the upper floors but the ground floor facade was demolished in the 1980s to make way for shops.

bylaws, it will have a more salutary effect and the barrow boys' rowdiness will be quelled."

Two years later, the problem was still so bad that the police organised "swoops" on vendors pitched without permission at the junction of Union Street and Wood Street. The culprits were forced not only to remove their barrows but to clear the streets of their crates and boxes. A fortnight later, there were more police raids and seven traders were taken away in a Black Maria. Ten traders were charged with obstruction.

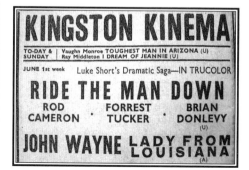

An advert for Kingston Kinema, Clarence Street, in June 1953 which appeared in the Surrey Comet.

Plain-clothed police prepare to move a barrow boy's vegetable stall in Church Street on 12th February 1955 after complaints of noise.

Advertisements which appeared in the pages of the Surrey Comet in June 1953.

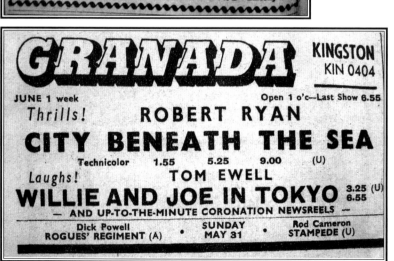

The latest 'must-haves' in 1953...

4 OUTSTANDING OFFERS!

In 1953, many people still did not have television and the radio was the focal point of many a living room.

Washout weather in the Fifties

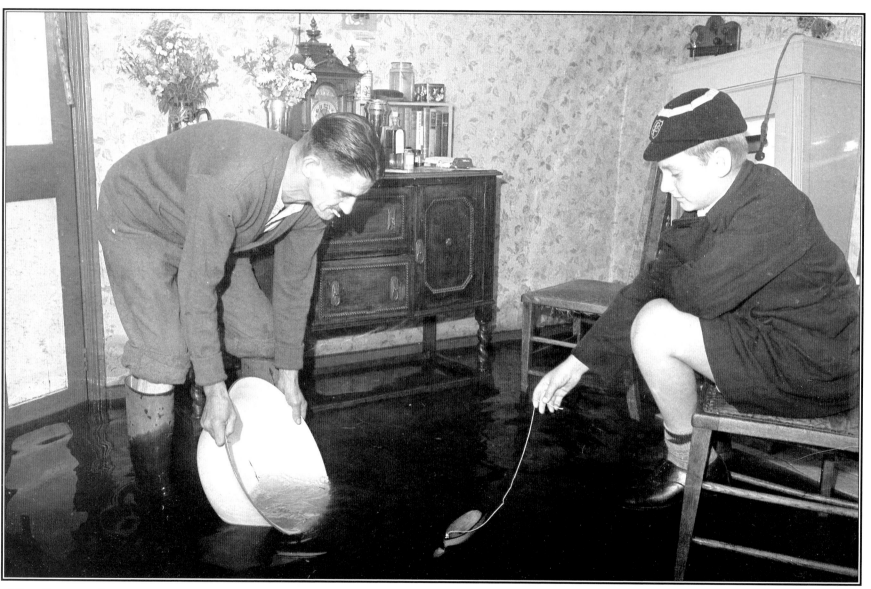

IN 1957 Kingston suffered what was then its wettest day on record.

The deluge began between 3 and 4pm on August 12.

After a respite it resumed at dawn the next day, flooding the town with more than three inches of rain in under 18 hours.

The Elm Road area of Canbury was worst hit when water flooded down from Richmond Park, bringing sand and silt which blocked gullies. Kingston Council gave householders disinfectant to cleanse their sewage-soaked floorboards, and sent men to collect sodden carpets for drying in the boiler room of the Coronation Baths in Denmark Road.

The Surrey Comet reported how three inches of rain fell in Kingston during the afternoon of Monday 12th August 1957 and the early hours of the following morning. Albert Fell, of Elm Road, had spent five hours drying out his home after the deluge only to find it under six inches of water hours later. As Mr Fell bales out the parlour, his young son seizes the chance to float his toy boat. The 1950s suffered a run of cool, disappointing summers until 1959 which was a hot one.

Flooded Elm Road on 13th August 1957, where a man prods vainly at a blocked drain. The exteriors of the houses on the right survive mostly unchanged. The main difference is that the shops in the distance are now dwellings. The prominent white building on the far left is the Wych Elm pub, which still flourishes.

Brigadier G.R.P. Roupell VC, colonel of the East Surrey Regiment, carried out the final inspection before the last passing out parade at Kingston Barracks, Kings Road, on 1st May 1959 following the East Surrey's merge with the Queen's Royal Surrey Regiment. Between 1875 and 1959 countless thousands of men trained as soldiers at the barracks, including 84,000 voluntary recruits during the First World War.

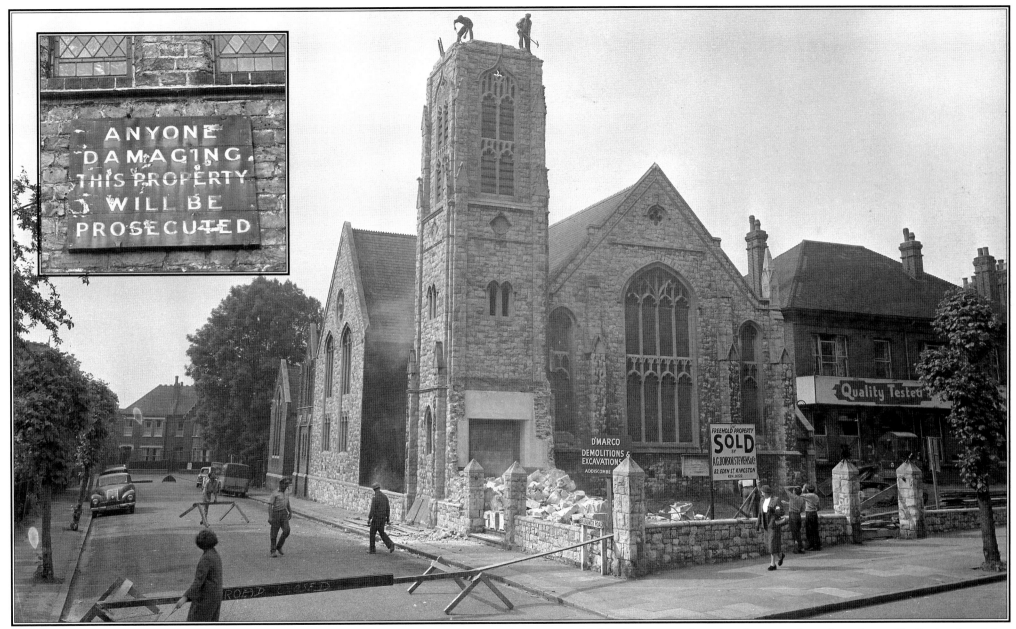

Demolition of the Kingston Hill Methodist Church, Brunswick Road, in May 1959. Inset: an ironic sign on the church wall. Strict health and safety rules like those of today were unheard of at this time. There are no screens to protect passers-by from falling masonry and no safety harnesses for the fearless workmen atop the tower. An office block now stands on this site. The building on the right, once a private house, had by the time of this picture become part of Kingston Hill Motor Works. A block of flats later replaced the premises.

Coronation street parties as Elizabeth is crowned in June 1953

Kingston's mayor, Alderman Geoffrey Lines, called in at a fancy dress party in Brunswick Road.

Two hungry young guests at the Clifton Road street party.

Street parties were held on 2nd June 1953 to mark the coronation of Queen Elizabeth II. This was the scene in Rosebery Road, Norbiton.

WIND and cold rain failed to dampen the enthusiasm of Kingston and Norbiton people in marking the crowning of Princess Elizabeth on 2nd June 1953. Street parties were held in Clifton Road, Brunswick Road, Rosebery Road and many other places and a parade was held through the town.

The new Queen had taken over the throne upon the death of her father, King George VI, the previous year but the coronation was held a year later to allow plans for the special occasion to be prepared.

Not far from Kingston, a crowd of 20,000 saw the young Queen when she came to Hampton Court with the Duke of Edinburgh and Princess Margaret for the Household Brigade ball. The large congregation of people cheered her, "a radiant figure in her diamond tiara, diamond necklace and white fur cape," reported the Surrey Comet.

Thousands across the borough watched the coronation in their own or neighbours' living rooms, using a modern media – black and white television.

Kingston's mayor and mayoress at a happy Coronation party in Clifton Road.

Street festivities in Burritt Road, Norbiton.

These "bathing beauties" took part in a procession in town.

Bonner Hill Road school was the venue for the Mill Place tea party.

Above: The Steadfast cadets fire three volleys at the moment of cremation.
Below: The solemn procession enters Bonner Hill Cemetery.

The new Lloyds Bank building, Clarence Street, in March 1959. It typified the post-war style of commercial architecture. Lloyds bank was the first occupant of Clarence Parade, which replaced the King's Arms after it closed in Clarence Street in 1956.

Kingston's Steadfast Sea Cadets march through the town with the coffin of their Lieutenant Commander W.J. Muddock, in July 1957. In the top picture the cortege emerges from Fairfield West, renamed Wheatfield Way, when it became part of the relief road in the 1980s. The shops on the left, including Bob Simester's store, patronised by many Scouts and Guides, were demolished at the same time.

Steadfast Cadets' funeral procession 1957

THE Steadfast Sea Cadets, formed in 1912, had become one of Britain's foremost Sea Cadet units in the 1950s, and the Lieutenant Commander W.J. Muddock was deemed worthy of a send-off with full military honours at his funeral held on 3rd July 1957.

It began at Frederick W Paine's chapel of rest in Fairfield West, where Lt Cdr Muddock's coffin, draped in the union flag and bearing his cap, sword belt and sword, was carried out to the waiting gun carriage by six sea cadets. The carriage was drawn by 32 cadets and taken through the town in a large procession to Kingston Crematorium where marine cadets fired three volleys at the moment of cremation. A funeral of such a grand scale is thought to be unique in the town.

Steadfast Sea Cadets gave their Sub-Lieutenant Geoffrey Southam full traditional naval honours when he married Joyce Fisher on 30th July 1956. After the service at Kingston Parish Church, the bridal pair stepped into a festooned car drawn by a gun carriage team of junior cadets. Headed by the Steadfast Band, the procession then made its way to a wedding breakfast at Steadfast's HQ on Thameside, watched by hordes of delighted spectators all the way. This picture shows the crowd in Thames Street. Behind them is the Jewellers & Silvermiths Co., which traded at the premises from 1878 to 1984. The building is now home to a milk bar, Shakeaway, and children's boutique, Peppermint.

Surbiton Lagoon

THERE can be hardly a family living locally that will not look back at Surbiton Lagoon with great affection and fond memories. Opened in Raeburn Avenue, Berrylands, in 1934, it was a top local attraction over the following 45 years during the summer months. Thousands flocked to the open air pools, fountains, and cafe where many a romance began. It closed "for repairs" in 1979 and never reopened. Houses and a small park are now on the site.

Left: Queues of people snake towards Surbiton Lagoon, one of the top summer attractions in the area. This was the scene on a hot day in June 1957. But the Fifties generally suffered from a run of cool and disappointing summers.
***Above**: A young swimmer gets a helping hand.*

The heyday of Surbiton Lagoon. Hundreds enjoy the holiday-like atmosphere at the attraction in August 1953.

Youngsters at Surbiton Lagoon keep cool in the hot summer of 1959. The photo was taken in August. On 5th July, temperatures hit 91F.

Surbiton Lagoon was the summer hot spot . . .

Above: *Detail from the earlier picture showing some of those in the long queue of people waiting to get into Surbiton Lagoon on a hot day in June 1957.* **Opposite:** *Fifties' lads at the lagoon in 1957.*

SUCH was the popularity of Surbiton Lagoon, in Raeburn Avenue, Berrylands, that on scorching hot summer days, like those in 1959, long queues of users formed at the gates.

Thousands would arrive from miles around to enjoy the holiday-like atmosphere at the lido.

Surbiton Lagoon was built on 20 acres of land in 1933. The site had been acquired by Surbiton Urban District Council in 1930 and the lagoon remained open until 1979.

One of the first managers was Edward Temme, who held a record for swimming the Channel. He swam the 38 miles from South Foreland to Blanc Nez, near Calais, in 15 hours and 54 minutes in August 1934. He was also the first man to swim the Channel both ways.

Two years before it closed, Princess Alexandra planted a silver birch at the lagoon. The ceremony was in January 1977 and marked the planting of a total of 25 trees to commemorate the Queen's silver jubilee.

The princess used a ceremonial silver spade owned by the Royal Borough of Kingston. The spade had been used by the mayor, Dr W. St Lawrence Finny, to plant a tree in Canbury Gardens on Coronation Day – 9th August 1902, close to the site of Kingston's former power station near the riverfront.

In these pictures note the young men's hairstyles which reflected the early rock'n'roll fashions set by the likes of Bill Haley whose 1955 hit Rock Around the Clock is as popular today at parties than it was more than 50 years ago. The "kiss curl" was much in vogue.

Other books by Mark Davison in this series

How to obtain these titles

Mark Davison

About the authors

JUNE SAMPSON has been features editor of the Surrey Comet since 1974, and much of her local history research has appeared in that paper. Her previous books include *The Story of Kingston* (1972); *Characters of Kingston* (1974); *Hidden Kingston* (1975); *Guide to Kingston Old Town Conservation Area* (1976); *All Change* (1985 and 1991); *Kingston and Surbiton Old and New* (1992); *Kingston Past* (1997); *Paintings of a Changing Kingston* (2004); and *The Kingston Book* (2006).

June Sampson – in the 1950s

She has been engaged in journalism and PR all her working life and has won many awards for professional achievements. She was judged Britain's top provincial journalist in property and townscape affairs for three consecutive years, and has twice been honoured with the Mayor of Kingston's Award for Outstanding Services to the Royal Borough.

MARK DAVISON worked on the Kingston Borough News after leaving Rivermead School, Kingston, and instantly acquired a love of local history.

He has written for the Surrey Mirror in Reigate for more than two decades.

His first of 20 books, *Surrey in the Hurricane*, published a year after the Great Storm of 1987 was a county bestseller, as was *Surrey in the Sixties*.